Meditation: the incredible gateway to an abundant life

Also by Jain Wells

Luminosity One – 2 CD set meditation album offering audio instruction for mindfulness meditation, and guided imagery visualization to support the integration of mindfulness into daily life, with music by Grammy and Emmy-award winning producer Kipper - utilizing brainwave synchronization entrainment to assist in understanding and experiencing meditative states that yield present-moment awareness and its infinite practical and spiritual benefits. This is available on iTunes and on Amazon.

To Be Real – Jain's pop music CD expresses her personal life experiences and the perspective of mindful living. Produced by Greg Fitzgerald. This is available on iTunes and Amazon.

www.drjainwells.com

www.jainwells.com

www.twitter.com/jainwells

www.facebook.com/jainwells

JAIN WELLS PhD

Meditation: the Incredible gateway to an abundant life

CHOICELESS AWARENESS, LONDON UK

This book is dedicated to those who are searching for greater meaning, purpose and joy in their lives and are willing to take steps to create that for themselves.

CONTENTS

PREFACE — i

CHAPTER ONE — Page 1
What Meditation Is And What It Isn't

CHAPTER TWO — Page 11
Types of Meditation

CHAPTER THREE — Page 29
Personal Growth and Spiritual Transformation

CHAPTER FOUR — Page 55
Guided Imagery Visualizations

CHAPTER FIVE — Page 75
Sitting Practices: Basic Steps

Published by Choiceless Awareness Records Ltd, London UK

ISBN 978-0-9576605-0-2

© Copyright 2013, Choiceless Awareness Records Ltd., London UK

All rights reserved. No part of this book may be reproduced in any form without written permission from the publisher.

Book design by Breeze Design, Guildford, UK
Photography: Howard Stern

Printed by Opal Print, Bath, UK
First edition June, 2013

The material used in this publication is, FSC Certified and Carbon Balanced. By using this material, 607kgs of carbon has been saved and 50.99sq. metres of land has been preserved.

www.carbonbalancedpaper.com

CBP00040862105134300

PREFACE

Meditation has long been associated with spirituality and the exploration of the higher dimensions of human existence and search for the meaning of life. If we fail to include this aspect in our overall development, it is easy to get caught in the illusions of life and the perception of separateness and struggle. The realm of experience itself is only possible through the spectrum of opposites. Through the contrast of light and dark, the whole picture or structure of experience is revealed. We need two legs to walk.

When we can acknowledge and reconcile this polarity within ourselves, and learn to dance with it, we become whole – warts and all. Through the highs and the lows we evolve and transform and mature. Meditation helps cultivate mindfulness in how we live and in who we are, beyond 'the story' we have constructed for ourselves based on a myriad of influences the moment we are born.

Meditation helps us to step back from our automatic and conditioned responses to life to observe, to respond mindfully, and to appreciate the beauty of the spectrum of experience. Through the understanding of our human nature we discover the divine qualities of self-forgiveness and compassion. These are our best solutions to living well.

I do not belong to any religious group or esoteric following, and do not want to create one, though I acknowledge the

PREFACE

wisdom found in most all major traditions. My doctorate is in the field of transpersonal psychology, which is a blend of the wisdom of those ancient traditions with the amazing discoveries and tools of Western psychology. In particular, I found myself attracted to practices that may be used to enhance personal and evolutionary development. Meditation is one such practice that I believe holds an important key to human understanding and evolution. It is my intent to help make the practice and benefits of meditation known to more people in service to individual and collective expansion. It truly is transformative.

JAIN WELLS - LONDON, UK - MARCH 11TH, 2013

What is necessary to change a person is to change his awareness of himself

ABRAHAM MASLOW

CHAPTER ONE

WHAT MEDITATION IS AND WHAT IT ISN'T

The practice of meditation is designed to quiet the activity of the mind – the mental chatter or internal dialogue that accompanies most people's entire daily waking experience, unless of course they are aware of it and have learned to control it or simply be with it. You can learn through meditation to cultivate present-moment awareness and in turn bring that clarity and presence into your daily life the more you practice it. Present-moment awareness is distinguished from your thinking processes involving thoughts of the past and future, by holding your focus on what is happening 'now'. The benefits from this are numerous.

Meditation accelerates healing on countless levels from a medical-physiological perspective, and from a personal growth and spiritual perspective. It's not just about "relaxing" – and there's nothing wrong with knowing how to do that either, though that is an understatement. It's so much more than that. While meditation induces a state of relaxation, sitting down and relaxing in the usual ways you might do that is not meditation. It is a state of mind that deepens your connection with yourself and others, and helps you to develop an attitude of non-judgement.

There is much confusion around what meditation actually is because it cannot be known intellectually, as a concept; it is known through experience. It is a practice that yields a unified state of awareness that transcends the mind's dualistic conceptual framework of a subject-object split (a world of separate objects).

CHAPTER ONE

As a teacher and practitioner of meditation for many years, I have had numerous conversations with people who say they meditate. Yet it is clear in our discussion of their experiences that something is missing in their understanding of what the practice truly involves. It is often the case that their attempts to meditate are either not sufficiently focused or consistent enough to allow a true meditative state to kick in, in order to tap its benefits. These discussions have also included a confusion of sleep or a pre-sleep state with meditation. This couldn't be further from the reality of the practice. Only the most advanced long-term meditators, often monks, can actually go into a sleep state and remain completely alert and awake, and that is a rarity.

That is why I highly recommend learning to meditate while sitting and not lying down, at least initially, as lying down and closing your eyes can be a tempting invitation to take a nap. Don't short change yourself by thinking you are engaged in the most amazing and beneficial practice, when you are completely 'checked out' as opposed to being razor-sharp in the present moment.

And then there are the excuses. Here are some of the comments I hear: "It's hard for me to meditate for very long because I get distracted," or "I can't sit still," or "I am too busy to meditate". The best one is, "I am too stressed to meditate". What do you think the meditation is for? It is to learn to quiet your mind from distraction, to help you learn to be still and to help you de-stress. Being human is not an easy ride, and yet we really do have all the resources within us to heal, grow and evolve.

CHAPTER ONE

The point of the practice is to remain committed to it so that you break through the initial barriers of distraction and discomfort to experience even a few seconds of 'quiet mind'. The toughest stage is at the beginning and that is why it is critical to learn to meditate in a quiet place. It doesn't matter how distracted your meditations sessions are initially. The practice is having the intention to slow down, and putting the time and effort in to achieve an understanding of what meditation is, and what it isn't. As you begin to observe the activity of your mind you also begin to see the very nature of mind as an incessant thinking machine. As you observe it in action, both in and outside of your meditation practice, you can be more objective and less identified with it. With this awareness, your life perspective and choices automatically shift.

In order to meditate you have to know what it means to meditate, and for this you have to have the experience of it, which only comes through consistent practice. Consistency is key, even more than duration at first. With as little as five minutes a day, and working up to 10 and 15 minutes each week or two and so on, you will start to get the hang on if it and be on your way.

To new meditators, 10 minutes can feel like an eternity depending on the general level of mental busyness they unconsciously maintain. It can also be physically uncomfortable to sit still, and nearly impossible to calm their thinking process down. I think that is why so many people take up the practice only to quit through sheer frustration and physical discomfort. It would be like expecting a child who has just eaten a bag of candy to sit

CHAPTER ONE

down and focus. His desire to get up, move around, and think about things is a dominant impulse. Usually one's current life problems take up the mindshare of mental activity at any given moment.

While its important to keep building on your 'sitting meditation' practice, once you know how to do it, you can practice mini-meditations almost anywhere – on the bus, train, plane, at your office desk, against a tree or even for a minute while you are standing in line at the bank. When you understand how to meditate you can use that skill to instantly help you centre yourself, and to simply acknowledge the blessing of being alive.

What's also very exciting is that meditation changes the course of your life. As you become more aware of yourself and your choices you can begin to consciously direct yourself as opposed to floating blindly down the river of life on a raft without a paddle. Only with an open and non-judgemental frame of mind do you become aware of the range of possibilities available to you. With consistency of practice and beginning with just a few minutes a day, it becomes do-able, and you build on it from there. When you have learned to train your mind to be still, it doesn't matter where you are or how busy or loud it is, the silence within is acknowledged.

My typical daily meditation session is 30 minutes in the morning when I wake up, and again for a certain period before I go to sleep. However, there are some busy or demanding days when I just get a few minutes to meditate wherever I am. In addition,

CHAPTER ONE

I try to meditate at least a couple of times a week for an hour or more at one time because I am aware of the amazing healing and growth benefits that regular deep sessions provide.
These are explained later in the book.

Suffice to say, there is no mistaking it when true 'quiet mind' arrives. It's just that so many people are not aware of the continual narration of their own mental ego chatter… that voice that won't stop analyzing, judgeing, comparing, worrying, and projecting one's own map of the world on to what is being seen and experienced.

Through meditation you activate your inner 'witness' or 'observer' and learn to re-direct your mental focus and maintain a position of non-judgement. When you can separate yourself from this ongoing internal dialogue and even watch it in action from an objective vantage point, a new stage emerges. This 'awakened' stage brings forth its gifts as present-moment awareness is sustained inside and outside of the meditation practice.

CHAPTER ONE

As a reference point for helping others learn to meditate I feel it helpful to make a distinction between what constitutes our Ego Self versus what we could call our Authentic Self. The word 'ego' is tossed around a lot in conversation often to refer to an inflated sense of self, i.e. John has a "big ego". The trouble with certain words however, is that they remain vague and unclear unless you specifically define what they are or at least what you mean to convey when using that word in a particular context.

For the purposes of discussion and understanding I will define these two terms in the way that they are referenced throughout this book. The Ego Self I define here as any variation of disturbance you might experience. This includes hate, anger, jealousy, self-doubt, greed, frustration, loneliness, uncertainty, judgement, competition, anxiety, and guilt, etc. This definition also includes the commonly used reference of 'ego' as an inflated sense of self as self-importance actually springs from insecurity. The Authentic Self, on the other hand, is when you are in a state of acceptance and peacefulness. By 'acceptance' I mean that you are acknowledging things as they are in the moment, and you are at peace within.

CHAPTER ONE

Manifestation and Growth

AUTHENTIC SELF EXPRESSION/VIBRATION

- Our natural state of being
- Acceptance, peacefulness and love
- Non-judgement
- Free-flowing energy
- Heightened awareness
- Interconnectedness of things, events, perception
- Clarity
- Self-acceptance and self-compassion
- Feeling of wholeness
- Manifestation and Growth

MOMENT OF CHOICE

Energy Drain and Need for Shifting

EGO SELF EXPRESSION/VIBRATION

- Disassociation from the Authentic Self, resulting in fear
- Fear expressed through lower realm emotions including: hate, anger, jealousy, self doubt, greed, frustration, loneliness, uncertainty, judgement, competition, anxiety, guilt, and self-importance etc.
- Disturbance in energy system
- Self-limiting beliefs
- Confusion
- Self-judgement and non-acceptance of self
- Feeling the need for protection
- Energy Drain and Need for Shifting

CHAPTER ONE

Through the practice of meditation and the cultivation of 'quiet mind' you strengthen your connection with your essential authentic nature and learn to detach from your ego reactions – ego reactions that spring from disturbance and resisting things as they are in any given moment. In the act of sustaining 'quiet mind' in your meditation practice, you train your mind to be less reactive and more objective in daily life as well. The meditation becomes you, and you become it.

Awareness automatically breeds more conscious choices simply because you see and notice things more, and have more options available to you. Reacting to something you don't like doesn't make it better. In fact, it often makes things worse and compounds the problem at hand. Learning to detach and become more objective gives you added clarity to help you make a more informed choice in any situation because it helps you to gain greater perspective. If you are freaking out you are not likely to make the best choice. On the other hand, if you are able to observe a situation that might otherwise have caused you to react, you can glide through the experience, take appropriate action as needed and save yourself the grief of reacting and feeling disturbed. How you deal with the issue is the issue.

To conclude, the act of quieting the mind for sustained periods of time through meditation sets in motion an incredible chain of events at all levels of your being. We know through scientific research and personal experience that it has a wide range of physical, mental, emotional and spiritual benefits that accumulate

CHAPTER ONE

with time. And back to my earlier statement about meditation as an experience and not an intellectual exercise: only through practice can you open and explore this amazing evolutionary gateway to an abundant life.

CHAPTER TWO

TYPES OF MEDITATION

Sitting Meditation Practices

Meditation is an ancient yogic practice. Its origins are rooted in most major spiritual traditions and encompass a variety of forms and styles. Meditation is being embraced by a greater number of people for its benefits at the mental, emotional, physical and spiritual levels.

There are many types of meditation practice though the main principle in each form is the same: it pertains to where and how you place your attention, or present-moment awareness. There are various types of meditation with different goals and qualities, which are important to understand if you are going to engage in the practice and get the results that you desire.

Sitting meditation has different effects on the body-mind than what I would call 'activity-based' meditations. Sitting meditation helps you cultivate the ability to quiet your mind and to achieve profound states of awareness that broaden your perspective of yourself and the nature of reality. This increasing awareness also enhances the quality of your experiences and your ability to make more conscious choices.

In addition to that, you can expand your mindfulness with a variety of activity-based meditations that consciously help you blend your world of action with the intention of remaining aware of yourself. While activity-based meditations are absolutely life-changing due to the fact that they increase awareness,

CHAPTER TWO

they do not replace the core practice of a sitting meditation that allows for other levels of depth not available in the activity-based practices on their own.

Sitting meditation, when practiced properly and consistently, allows the practitioner to achieve deep meditative states of awareness with particular results that are unique. In the Eastern traditions there are two main types of sitting meditation, each with a distinct approach: one form is 'receptive' and the other is 'concentrative', and each form has defining characteristics.

Mindfulness meditation, known as Vipassana in the Buddhist tradition, is 'receptive'; it trains the mind to rest in the present moment while allowing various objects of experience to also be present in a non-focused way. For example, it is common in mindfulness meditation to loosely hold your attention on the inflow and outflow of your breath (as the act of breathing is ever-present), yet when a thought comes to mind, it is gently acknowledged while the attention is returned to the breathing (to the present). Similarly, there could be sounds in the environment, though they do not become the focal point of one's attention. The idea is to hold a receptive and open state of mindfulness on the present moment without fixating or focusing on anything in particular, and allowing all sounds, thoughts and sensations to arise and dissolve into the present moment without judgement or fixation. For this reason, mindfulness meditation is said to give rise to insight as it creates a space within you for anything to arise and to be seen.

CHAPTER TWO

It also brings awareness to the characteristic of the mind to want to think and keep thinking. It is so easy to completely identify with your thoughts that you don't even know that a reality beyond thinking even exists. This alternate reality is that of Authentic Self expression and the qualities of acceptance and peacefulness. It is differentiated, as explained in chapter one, from Ego Self expression and the variety of conditioned states and disturbances other than acceptance and peacefulness.

The mindfulness practice is training for the mind to slow down, so that you may rest in 'quiet mind'. On different days you may have more mental chatter than others. Yet with consistent practice your ability to slow your thinking down and rest in stillness will improve. Eventually if you want to take your practice deeper you will have to learn to achieve that stillness in a sustained way. At this point your actual brainwave frequency slows down and yields another level of benefits. Like anything, with practice you get better at it. It is critical to remember however, that the point of the practice is to quiet the mind and not to follow or fixate on ideas.

I once suffered from a temporary physical injury in one of my hip joints that had a perpetual throbbing pulsation of pain. When I sat to meditate and began to place my attention on my breathing I was able to keep my awareness on the steady rhythm of the pulsating pain as well as on my breath and managed to integrate the pain into the practice. My field of awareness held both objects of experience in a relaxed, unfixed way. I allowed the pain to become part of the meditation interplay in the

CHAPTER TWO

moment without allowing my mind to analyze or think about the pain. It was simply another 'instrument' in the song.

Quite often I will begin my practice with mindfulness and move into concentrative practice, which is essentially opposite in approach to mindfulness meditation.

'Concentrative' meditation is another form of mental training that pertains to the practice of holding one's attention on a sound, object, image or idea with single-pointed focus. Transcendental Meditation (TM) was introduced in the West from India in the 1950's. It is a form of concentrative practice that specifically uses mantra (the repetition of a sound or phrase) to induce a meditative state.

In Buddhism and other yoga systems of India it is known as the basic practice of Samatha. Many Buddhists start with Samatha to get concentration and one-pointedness and then switch to Vipassana or receptive meditative practice.

Holding one's unwavering focus on a sound, object, idea or image leads to the experience of absorption, whereby the practitioner has the experience of feeling one with the object of experience. Unlike mindfulness training your attention is completely fixated on the sound, object or image without distraction. Similar to mindfulness meditation, you are completely centred in the present moment. Both concentrative and mindfulness forms of meditation involve steady practice to centre the mind in the present moment, working with distractions, yet one's attention is centred in very different way in order to cultivate

CHAPTER TWO

'quiet mind'.

All forms of meditation have a positive impact on awareness. That is their purpose. I combine both receptive and concentrative forms into my practice. A key point I would like to emphasize when considering taking up the practice of meditation is to include a form of sitting meditation as your core practice, and ideally combining both approaches. The sitting meditations allow space for greater depth of awareness and transformation to occur, penetrating to increasing levels of depth over a lifetime.

Present-Moment Awareness

As you will read in chapter three, meditation has many measureable benefits pertaining to health, healing, personal growth and spiritual awareness. Cultivating present-moment awareness is the gateway to activating those greater human potentials. So what does present-moment awareness actually mean and how does that feel? It means that you are aware of yourself in any given moment; your thoughts, feelings, bodily sensations, sounds, and objects in your immediate environment. It also means that you are free from chasing thoughts about the past and future to be in the now with what is happening. As you continue your practice you will begin to feel lightness in your being, allowing you to be more calm, open, free and spontaneous. At different times the practice will unearth emotions or memories and help you to integrate them, ultimately opening you up to a greater range of self-expression. As your Authentic

CHAPTER TWO

Self shines through with increasing energy into your daily life, your Ego Self reactions are minimized. This is personal and spiritual growth.

Non-Judgement

The practice of non-judgement is synonymous with meditation. It is another aspect of mental training that improves with practice. Non-judgement is the act of observing something as it is, without needing or wanting to judge it or place a value or meaning on it as either "good" or "bad". Refraining from judging something broadens your awareness and offers you a wider range of potential perspectives and responses. In the same way that we observe a thunderstorm and a bolt of lightning that hits something as an occurrence, even though it may bring destruction, we can bring that same level of objectivity to other life events. In doing so, we can maintain a greater sense of equilibrium and objectivity that not only enhances our feelings of peacefulness, it allows us to take action, when needed, with greater awareness and efficiency. Emotional reactions are often uncomfortable and non-productive.

When we are centred in a state of non-attachment we remain in the present-moment, free from riding the mental and emotional highs and lows that accompany judgement. We do the tough training in the meditation practice and allow this training to permeate our daily lives, becoming less reactive and more compassionate and sensitive to others who may not know how

CHAPTER TWO

not-to-react.

The Unconscious Mind

The most profound aspect of meditation for me has involved coming into an understanding of its relationship with the unconscious mind, and how consistent practice begins to make one increasingly 'conscious' of what has been hidden from awareness… at multiple levels. This includes habits, addictions, limiting beliefs, defense mechanisms, unconscious desires and motivations, fears and repressed memories. These postures affect your ability to express yourself freely and fully.

In fact, the layers of depth of the human psyche and the ego structure versus the experience of Authentic Self-expression are much more involved and advanced than this beginner's book on meditation allows. Suffice to say, it is my hope that these distinctions I am making between the different types of meditative practices and how they affect the body-mind will help others gain the necessary understanding of the practice in order to do it properly to allow them to penetrate those structures as deeply as they choose throughout the course of their lives. At a certain point, you must learn to calm your mental chatter to rest in sustained 'quiet mind' in order to move into those increasing layers of depth.

Meditation draws unconscious and subconscious content to the foreground of your awareness and allows you to see it. You may simply observe it and take note, or it may bring up content that may be difficult or uncomfortable for you to look at. Different

CHAPTER TWO

things will need to be integrated at a different pace. It can be alarming or disturbing to shine light on what you may not want to see and acknowledge about yourself, ie. a habit that you haven't be willing to address may become more prominent or an issue that you have been in denial about becomes painfully obvious – prompting you to make a more self-honouring choice. How you integrate this content is up to you. There are no limits to self-discovery.

If an emotion comes up during a meditation session, this is a marvelous thing. It also means you are on the right track. We are feeling beings. Often an emotional memory or experience that you have had simply wants to be felt, and that is all that is needed to integrate it. Other times, it will provide 'food for thought' over a period of time, allowing you to observe and integrate it at your own pace. Denying an issue simply perpetuates it. You may also decide to seek the counsel of a therapist to assist you in working through a tough emotional issue.

Crying is one of the body's great functions for processing emotions. Just let yourself feel the emotion and remember to keep breathing. Holding or choking your breath is a defense mechanism that will keep you stuck and unaware as it impedes the flow of energy. Whatever you deny or resist prevents you from moving forward into greater self-expression. When you are experiencing unpleasant emotions, it is helpful to feel the emotions consciously and move into the act of self-forgiveness and compassion as these are also attributes of the Authentic Self

CHAPTER TWO

and may assist you to shift a disturbance. This is an immensely powerful tool, if you can develop the ability to practice it at will. Simply allow yourself to feel compassion for the part of you that is feeling vulnerable, regardless of the circumstances. There is always room for self-forgiveness.

Meditation will help you become more aware of yourself, more aware of the hidden aspects of your ego-personality, let go of attitudes that no longer serve you or have meaning, and put you in touch with the 'real' authentic you that is not defined by your life conditioning.

As meditation connects you with your authentic self, the idea of healing is ultimately a healing of your own perspective of yourself and a dissolving of the many layers of ego conditioning that served to separate you from authenticity; your essential nature of acceptance and peacefulness. Imagine who you would be and what you could embrace in life without your current fears?

Meditation serves to strip away the conditioning and unconscious associations you have developed in life and to perceive them with greater clarity and objectivity. That is why the practice of mindfulness meditation is said to lead to insight as the inner stance of your open unfixed awareness allows for many thoughts, feelings and sensations to arise. Meditation is incredibly healing for this reason.

Having made these points about the association between emotion and meditation, certain individuals may not be suited to the practice of sitting meditation for a variety of reasons.

CHAPTER TWO

If someone is in a state of denial about their current life experiences, or using substances as a way of "checking out" of the realities of daily life, meditation may simply become another crutch to escape from living-in-the-world. As well, someone suffering from psychological issues or lacking the grounding and ability to cope within daily life, wouldn't necessarily be suited to the practice of meditation either. On the other hand, if you are ready to grow and expand, meditation will assist in helping you to re-balance and integrate feelings of discomfort and to make new self-affirming choices.

Objective Reality

From the perspective of your outer-world reality, meditation serves to strip away the conditioning and blind identification you have with certain objects of experience. As you learn to train yourself to hold this centred and objective inner stance, your perception of yourself and your relation to others and the world changes with it. Imagine hearing a sound simply as a sound, as opposed to a sound that is associated with something. For example, can you hear the sound of an airplane in flight or the sound of a blender as just sounds as opposed to being sounds that an object that you have previously experienced is creating?

If you are feeling connected with the importance and benefit of stepping back from situations in your life to view them more objectively, here is another step you can take in becoming more objective. Hearing the sound of a plane or a blender as a sound and not a sound-as-object isn't too tough. What about the sound of someone screaming? Couldn't this just be a sound as well?

Social Conditioning

How about your associations pertaining to social conditioning? How objective are you? Advertising is nothing more than conditioning you and influencing you to buy and get attached to using a particular product or service. There are countless other ways we become identified: by where we live, our gender, race, history and group belief systems. We may equally use this blind mode of identification to separate us from others who do not hold our values. How does this social conditioning limit your life experience?

Some things we may think are silly or don't make sense, and other aspects may hit our value system and make us feel in judgement. While you may not agree with a particular way of thinking, the more calm and centred you are the more likely you can learn to observe with understanding and compassion. This is the path to positive change.

One of the interesting effects of Internet communication is how it increases our knowledge of other cultures: what they believe and how they live. Through this awareness comes understanding and tolerance. Of course there is less tolerance for other cultures that degrade or abuse others, though that doesn't mean we have to dislike them for it. Cultural values are deeply rooted with all sorts of rationale behind them. We can understand that others have been conditioned to respond in certain ways as we have.

CHAPTER TWO

It is a little more difficult to step outside of one's own cultural conditioning than it is to identify and observe the differences in other cultures.

Meditation works at this level as well, to help you centre in your Authentic Self, and view the range of life expression with its highs and lows that need not be "good" and "bad". After all, it is the spectrum of life experience that allows for one thing to be viewed in contrast to something else, and therefore to be experienced. Life and death and everything in between are equally beautiful when we see that it is the whole system of life that has blessed us with the ability to experience at all. Similarly, the highs and lows represent our pain, pleasure and opportunity for growth.

Seeing with new eyes and an open mind can only enhance your ability to remain calm and to experience life more fully and fluidly. Non-judgement is a skill that can be learned.

Choiceless Awareness

A significant part of this meditation book explains the benefits of meditation as supporting greater awareness and making more conscious choices. It is about living more consciously. The term choiceless awareness however, pertains to a state of consciousness beyond the push and pull of choice. It is not defined by the need to choose or to take action, rather to be present in a state of pure awareness beyond the impulse of needing anything. It naturally involves the act of non-judgement, observing things as they are, and remaining so present in the

CHAPTER TWO

moment that you transcend the impulse of choice itself.

Certainly we are beings of action in the world and I do believe in taking personal responsibility for one's creations and seeking open-mindedness that may yield consciously intended experiences. When you are 'in the moment' you notice things. If you are mentally or emotionally distracted, you miss information, are less aware and hence make less-informed choices.

With continued meditative practice, your relationship to maintaining present moment awareness and the nature of choice itself will certainly evolve. Even to observe the impulse of choice within you and to observe yourself acting on that impulse is a valuable practice. You will begin to notice how many automatic responses you have to ideas, words, situations or people due to previous conditioning and limited awareness. We can learn to unlearn those responses and remain more open, spontaneous and creative in life.

Other terms that you may hear that are synonymous with choiceless awareness are non-dual awareness or witness consciousness.

Osho succinctly states this distinction:

When the witness arises, there is nobody who is witnessing and there is nothing to be witnessed. It is a pure mirror, mirroring nothing.

CHAPTER TWO

Activity-based Practices

The activity-based practices represent mindfulness in action, in conscious interaction with your outer experience so that you are 'doing' and 'being' with mindfulness. The intention is to be mindfully engaged in the sensory detail of the activity, whatever that is, while remaining present with yourself. It could be a meditation that involves holding love in your heart and directing it to others or washing the dishes with awareness. Imagine bringing your full attention to this task.

You scan the dishes to be washed. You reach for the plug and feel it in your fingers, wrapped around its edges with your grip, as you press it firmly it into the hole in the bottom of the sink, noting the pressure that is required to do this. You turn the water tap on noting the pressure needed to loosen the handle. You watch the water fall from the tap, and make adjustments as you sense into the changing temperature with the tips of your fingers.

You pick up and feel the soap container in your hands, noting its bright green colour, and you feel the tension created as you squeeze a few drops into the sink, hearing the sound of air that rushes from the half-empty bottle. A mushroom cloud of bubbles appears and with it the faint smell of pine, and the crackling of bursting bubbles. Every speck of food, its colour and texture, comes alive as it meets the scrub brush in your hand. No detail goes unnoticed as you bring your present-moment awareness to yourself in the activity.

CHAPTER TWO

Practitioners of meditation become more sensitive to life, to details that were previously unnoticed, are more open and trusting, less fearful and consequently less guarded. Do you remember the last time you had a conversation with someone and you knew they were thinking about something else instead of being present with you, listening to what you are saying and responding mindfully? Just think of how much of life's rich experiences you are missing by not being present. From the details in your work life that may hinder productivity to missing the new expressions of your two-year-old as he shares a new word, there is an endless stream of moments unfolding into life that is completely unique to your experience. How much are you really living in each moment?

HERE ARE SOME OTHER
MINDFULNESS ACTIVITIES YOU CAN TRY:

Mirror Gaze – take a few minutes and begin glancing into your own image in the mirror. Gently hold your gaze on your eyes while allowing all of your individual features to be present though not a focal point of your awareness. Your vision may go in and out of focus, so just let that be what it is. Similarly, any sensations and feelings that arise just let them blend into the overall experience of the moment. As thoughts arise, simply acknowledge them and return your full awareness to your eyes. You will naturally also be present with the inflow and outflow of your breath. Its rhythm may change and you simply observe.

CHAPTER TWO

Body Meditation – take three deep breaths of air… breathing in relaxation and exhaling tension (feel the energy move through your body) breathing in relaxation and exhaling tension (breathing deeply into your entire body) breathing in relaxation and exhaling tension. Continue breathing consciously placing your awareness on the inflow and outflow of your breath. Sense into an area of your body that is feeling tense or uncomfortable. It may be a sensation or an area that feels muscle tension, or energy of any kind. Where are you feeling this energy? How are you feeling it? Place your awareness on this area and continue to breathe 'life and healing' into that area. Note how conscious breathing immediately shifts your energy.

Heart Meditation – bring to mind a challenge you may be dealing with in your life today. Imagine an image of yourself as you are today or at any other time, consoling yourself around this challenge, as only you would know exactly what you would like that to be. Regardless of the circumstances of the situation, any discomfort you may be experiencing is real enough if you are feeling it. Just try it. Think of any difficult issue you are dealing with and allow yourself to be vulnerable with yourself, and open up to feel what you feel… whether it is anger, sadness, loss, physical pain etc. Let the feeling be felt and breathe in acceptance for that is how you are feeling in this moment, and glide into self-compassion. Imagine observing yourself consoling yourself. Breathe into that visual image and relax, breathe into that visual image and relax, breathe into that visual image and relax. Note how the honest feeling of self-compassion lightens your energy.

Walking Meditation – get yourself ready in comfortable clothing and go out for a meditation walk. Keep your awareness on your physical body and its movement. Be mindful of any past or future thoughts that arise and instantly shift your awareness to the sights, sounds, and textures around you melding into present moment experience. A walk in nature allows the walking awareness to be present with the aliveness of life all around. Hold the quality of gratitude in your heart as you observe. With continued practice you carry this present moment awareness into any activity, living and expressing from your Authentic Self while positively affecting your relationships, and your relationship to yourself. Practice feeling gratitude as you begin to take notice of the ways you feel blessed in this life.

CHAPTER THREE

PERSONAL GROWTH AND SPIRITUAL TRANSFORMATION

One of the many fascinating aspects about developing present-moment awareness through meditation is how your increased awareness can allow you to experience life more intimately. You gain the power and ability to consciously create and direct your experiences. By stepping back to observe yourself in action you simply start to notice things you did not notice before, and this creates an impetus to make different choices. The more facets of your life that you pay attention to – mental, emotional, physical and spiritual – the more you, and every aspect your life, accelerate and develop. Stimulating development in each of these areas aids personal growth and spiritual transformation. In that sense it is integral or all-inclusive of your overall human capacities.

For example, if you want to be the best you can be in this life – physically healthy, emotionally centered, mentally focused and spiritually aware – you have to make certain choices to develop in those areas. If you had a desire to become a professional athlete, you would seriously be limiting your chances of success if you did not know how to focus. You would also impair your performance if you paid no attention to nutrition. As well, if you are constantly struggling with emotional issues instead of addressing and healing them, it can be impossible to have clarity of mind and a balanced state of being, or to move forward on your plans, whatever they may be.

CHAPTER THREE

Personal growth has been shown to lead to spiritual awareness. My use of the word 'spiritual' simply refers to how I have been differentiating between the Ego Self (or conditioned self) versus the Authentic Self, which is free from judgement and rests in a state of acceptance and peacefulness of all experiences.

To reiterate one of my main points in the preface of this book: The realm of experience itself is only possible through the spectrum of opposites. Through the contrast of light and dark, the whole picture or structure of experience is revealed. Do we need to judge and resist the very structure that allows us to have experiences or can we embrace the beauty of it and the opportunity to grow and evolve? The highs and lows represent the path of movement and growth itself. Observing yourself and all of your experiences from a place of non-judgement allows you to connect with your Authentic Self; to break free from your identification with personal life challenges and conditioned responses to life. Mindfulness and present moment awareness without judgement is an integral part of embodied spirituality.

Transpersonal Psychology

The word 'transpersonal' means 'trans' or 'beyond' your personal or ego-personality self. Transpersonal psychology combines the transformative psychological principles of the Eastern, Western and indigenous wisdom traditions with the principles and tools of Western psychology. Thus the examination of our human potential gives rise to an awareness of our transcendent side in a new way… the essential human consciousness of each individual as pure awareness untouched by individual and social conditioning. What if we could align with that higher dimension of ourselves and remain awake to that knowing in the dream called 'life'? As Jungian analyst Marion Woodman aptly says, "Loving our crooked neighbor with our own crooked heart." The whole spectrum or range of human possibilities exists in each of us. Self-forgiveness, self-love and compassion are the pathway through this bumpy, beautiful ride called life. Meditation is one important practice that can help you ride through more purposefully and gracefully.

Note to readers: For the purpose of clarity, the word 'spiritual' will be used interchangeably with the word 'transpersonal' where appropriate.

My Research

The research I conducted as part of my doctoral education involved a combination of daily mindfulness meditation practice and weekly guided imagery visualizations over an 8-week period, beginning with 14 participants and ending with 11 who committed to and completed the practices. The data collection process involved the following:

1. A pre-study interview to determine each individual's general life situation, i.e. challenges, goals, life perspective.

CHAPTER THREE

2. Daily mindfulness meditation practices beginning with 10 minutes a day for two weeks, moving up to 15 minutes for four weeks, and concluding with 20 minutes for two weeks, and journaling their experiences each day around what they experienced.

3. Weekly guided imagery visualization exercises over the 8-week period around a variety subjects in order to bring up and stimulate content to work with, followed by journaling about their experiences.

4. A post-study interview to assess what kinds of changes, if any, took place.

All the data collected from these steps provided the content and context for the study, and the results I observed and reported. Their personal details have been altered slightly to maintain confidentiality.

Participant Profiles

Amy female 36, Allen male 37, Kent male 25, Jenny female 41, Eva female 42, Jim male 37, Joel male 29, Shannon female 38, Bonnie female 23, David male 30, and Frances female 34. With the exception of one of the female participants who referred to herself as a 'housewife', the other participants are self-sufficient individuals who work at regular 9 to 5 jobs, employed by other people. They were selected based on their general level of self-sufficiency and personal stability.

CHAPTER THREE

The Results

All 11 participants experienced significant personal growth such that they all made a range of personal life choices that enhanced their lives. These shared experiences of personal growth included varying degrees of issue resolution, feeling more calm and relaxed, less reactivity, enhanced sense of confidence and self-acceptance, increased ability to focus, enhanced organizational skills, and a greater level of openness with others. Other changes experienced by some of the participants from the group included increased desire for self-care and self-nurturing, enhanced ability to communicate, greater desire and ability to balance work and personal life, and greater insight into the nature of the mind.

Five of those 11 people reported having spiritual (transpersonal) experiences according to this definition as outlined in the study:

The word transpersonal refers to the aspect of human experience that transcends the ego-personality: A transpersonal experience is defined as an experience of altered states of consciousness beyond ordinary time/space awareness, the feeling of present-moment awareness, feelings of deep inner peace, feelings of blissfulness, and a sense of oneness or interconnectedness with objects of experience. This understanding includes a form of the transpersonal (spiritual) experience known as nondual awareness, which is a sense of oneness or underlying unity among the various aspects of reality.

In fact, the central question for the research was "Is the experience of personal growth and transpersonal experience

CHAPTER THREE

enhanced in the context of integral transformative practices* (stimulating growth through combined practices pertaining to mental, physical, emotional and spiritual dimensions of the self), and if so, how?" The participants were not aware of this intention so that they could engage freely and naturally with the practices.

It was interesting to note through the data that all of the spiritual experiences occurred during the daily mindfulness meditation practice, in the latter half of the 8-week study, and varied in frequency for each individual.

Another interesting point was the fact that 3 out of 6 participants who did not have a spiritual experience said that they preferred and benefited from the guided imagery exercises more so than from the mindfulness meditation. Paradoxically, those same 3 participants also said that they were surprised at how clearly and vividly they could visualize things. All but one of the 5 participants who did have spiritual experiences said they benefited equally from both practices, and that 1 individual participant said that he preferred the meditation practice for the simple reason that he didn't quite feel comfortable in the group dynamic.

These findings would seem to suggest, in the limited context of this study, that spiritual experiences may not necessarily occur with the use of guided imagery alone, without the practice of mindfulness meditation. I concluded through the assessment of the overall findings that those individuals who were able

CHAPTER THREE

to get beyond obsessive thinking in the meditation to experience more sustained periods of inner stillness opened themselves to spiritual awareness.

Experiences of Personal Growth

The guided imagery exercises were specifically designed to call up and help integrate various points of tension or challenge in the individual's life. The daily mindfulness meditation, in a less direct way, ultimately served this same function, and both practices supported each other toward this end. The following are some examples of personal growth experiences reported by the participants pertaining to both practices. For the sake of accuracy, the direct quotes have been retained. Some of the quotes are repeated in certain sections where multiple references are relevant.

Amy: "I realized what works for me and what doesn't. It's in my hands and in my heart." "I also closed the door on my old relationship. It was a part of life that was unhealthy." "Before I was insecure and didn't want to risk and show my feelings and be rejected. Now I can expose myself and express my feelings." "I am open to new people. I started to trust a bit more." "I was thinking today of being more accepting of who I am and not play somebody else."

Allen: "My love life—I am not complaining. I feel I am in the right place with myself. I feel like I feel more in control now as a result of the meditation." "I also feel more comfortable to approach

CHAPTER THREE

others and I don't feel shy or guilty." "My sister and I have completely new communication that wasn't there before." "Before starting the meditation I found it difficult to wake up. I have a lot more energy to start my meditation in the morning. Now I don't even feel like staying in bed."

Kent: "I haven't had any feelings of depression since doing this program." "There were quite a few past experiences that came up that helped me recognize why I have resistance to meeting new people." "He [the bird he visualized in one of the exercises] told me that sometimes it takes time for soul mates to find each other and that circumstances had to be just right for that to happen. That made sense to me. It's a matter of time. I feel that this is true."

Jenny: "I am starting to communicate differently with my daughter." "I imagined the old life being replaced by a new life and opening myself to explore another relationship." "I feel a sense of peace even though I have so many things to sort out." "I have noticed that I have stopped jumping into situations and remain quieter, waiting to see what happens."

Eva: "I would have been a blithering mess without the meditation. Ordinarily something like that [her difficult neighbor] could really upset me, and although it's upsetting I'm dealing with it." "I'm less passive-aggressive I suppose." "I want to get fit, I'm watching what I eat, and I am taking vitamins and eating really well, and watching my alcohol." "I think I am communicating better with people." "I am able to slow my thoughts down and express myself." "I really did embrace the fact that I can see things from other people's point of view."

Jim: "What I have come to realize is that all the resolution to those problems is all within me." "I have started saying 'yes' to more things." "I want to invest more effort in the rest of my life. It gave me ideas to do that." "I saw the bits about myself that I wasn't so pleased about, more clearly, like those slightly slovenly and lazy aspects of my character that I dislike. I think they are very easy to fix." "I also used to take things personally."

Joel: "I have developed a habit of breathing deeply whenever I think of it. I think that is a powerful tool for calming down." "I am definitely feeling more relaxed and I am moving more slowly than I did." "I can feel the difference between chaos and the joy of a still moment."

Shannon: "Its energy and assertiveness is making me feel reawakened and confident." "I am very positive and a lot calmer than I expected to be with such a big move. I am normally at the back of the list."

Bonnie: "I have got more control, and I'm a lot more calm about things." "It taught me a lot about my internal process—to slow down and think about things, and that it's okay to open up to things."

David: "I really don't worry that much anymore." "I started to realize that if I was organized and the not so fun stuff was taken care of then that allows me to concentrate on what's more important like my relationship and work." "I kind of learned to laugh at myself if stupid thoughts came into my head whereas before I got caught up."

Frances: "I feel like I am developing, whereas before I felt at a bit of a standstill." "My relationship seems to be better. My husband has noticed changes in me, very positive changes, and I'm very calm to be around now." "My anger is a lot better also. Even if someone gets me angry now or someone says something that makes me feel angry I try to put it aside." "Since I have been doing the meditation I started to focus on my body more."

Guided Imagery Exercises

The guided imagery exercise, as an integral transformative tool, was specifically chosen to assist an individual with issue resolution, in support of the assertion that this type of personal change could potentially remove blockages to allow a spiritual experience to occur. The issue resolution within this context took the form of producing insights and ideas that helped them with personal challenges, as well as for realizing their desires. It also brought up emotions around painful subjects for some of the participants, and provided an opportunity to help them heal and integrate those disturbances. The participants experienced issue resolution and/or significant insights during certain guided imagery exercises more than others.

The guided imagery exercises that appeared to have the greatest impact on most of the participants were exercises 1 (letting go), 2 (accessing inner wisdom), 5 (healing childhood memory), and

CHAPTER THREE

8 (desired experiences). Some participants were also greatly impacted by exercises 3 (working through challenging situation), 4 (acknowledging talent/life purpose), 6 (flexibility/balance in life), and 7 (releasing/inviting new quality).

The eight guided imagery exercises created for this study in the order as presented, were:

1. Loss (letting go/rebirth);

2. Observer (accessing inner wisdom);

3. Tree Meditation (working through challenging situation);

4. Talents (acknowledging talent/life purpose);

5. Inner Child (healing childhood memory);

6. Rhythm (flexibility/balance in life);

7. Ocean Wave (releasing/inviting new quality);

8. Future Vision (desired experiences).

These exercises are outlined in chapter four, for you to use and integrate into your own personal development work.

Here are some examples of how the guided imagery exercises elicited issue resolution. Amy: "When searching my inner wisdom I heard that God still loves me even if I witness some terrible scenes. I had this message that I am independent from it. It is only in the past and it is not part of my life at all. I was cuddling this little girl (herself as a child) and felt compassion for her."

CHAPTER THREE

Allen: "Today's meditation [visualization] was quite intense but more towards the end. I could feel the sense of achievement in the future. I could feel the presence of my family and friends in my life."

Kent: "The situation I thought about was feeling alone and not being able to find a soul mate to hang out with. The bird that flew on to the tree was a large colorful talking parrot. He told me that sometimes it takes time for soul mates to find each other and that circumstances had to be just right for that to happen. That made sense to me. It's a matter of time. I feel that this is true."

Jenny: "The one about the childhood memory was interesting. There was a situation with my mother when I was about 12 years old that came up. She embarrassed me in front of my friends at a school sports event and I hated her for that. She made me look stupid. I didn't talk to her after that for a while, and it put a wedge between us." Jenny made a significant comment in the post-study interview pertaining to that session. She felt that there was a "hint" of a parallel between her relationship with her mother and not feeling good enough and her own feelings of inadequacy around pleasing her daughter.

Eva: In reference to guided imagery exercise 2, she said, "And in the wise one where I really did embrace the fact that I can see things from other people's point of view. And that's what I am using now with the neighbor to counteract the problem we have—my ability to empathize. I can keep Jack from flying off the handle. At times he finds it hard and needs me around."

CHAPTER THREE

Jim: "There was one in particular [guided imagery exercise 1] where I was amazed at how quickly most of these thoughts went straight to dad. I was amazed how quickly these thoughts manifested." When he thought about the loss of his father and the high expectations he had of himself to please his father, a significant association came to mind regarding the fact that he and his wife had not currently been able to conceive. "Perhaps the reason that hasn't happened yet is my inability to believe in myself as the adult character. I remembered thinking, "You are the adult now and once you accept that you can be the father. Maybe that's something that is holding me back. And that felt kind of cleansing I must say."

Joel: In guided imagery exercise 3 he commented, "The bird I visualized was a raven. It told me that the reason my parents, and particularly my father, kept after me was because I didn't give them any time or anything of myself. The raven said that if I could make an effort to have a conversation with them and tell them what is happening in my life that they would feel better and withdraw. I realized that I had shut them out, and felt some sadness around this."

Shannon: From the eighth guided imagery exercise, she wrote, "I saw myself with children. It was just me with children. There was no male figure. You look at the things that you see. It's really amazing. It's a strange visualization because of not being in a stable relationship yet the children came into it and I felt them. The happiness in the visualization that I felt, it was really real, like actually physically being there."

CHAPTER THREE

Bonnie: Concerning guided imagery exercise 7, she commented, "The quality of insecurity came to mind, visualized as a black pebble on a flawless beach. When it washed away I imagined life to be calmer and carefree—more inner confidence. The second quality was that of being carefree. I didn't visualize an object as such but I could feel it travelling towards me on waves. I felt warm and tingly when it reached me. Life with this quality felt good and strong. People reacted well and this in turn made me feel more relaxed."

David: Regarding guided imagery exercise 3, he wrote, "I felt very connected to the tree and earth and the current situation between me and my girlfriend. I saw a big, strong eagle as my inner self and guide instructing me to remain strong and consistent and to be there for her but to give her space to think. It's the best thing I can do." From guided imagery exercise 5, he wrote, "You can be more assertive whilst staying true to yourself and your natural personality."

Frances: "I saw the talent [visualization 4] as a paint brush and I communicated with it. It made me feel happy when I imagined painting and doing artwork and putting it in a display in an exhibition. It made me feel happy and proud that people liked the bold and bright colors that I used, and gave me good feedback." This experience led her to sign up for a calligraphy course.

To reiterate, 3 out of 11 participants, who did not report having any spiritual experiences, said that they preferred and benefited

CHAPTER THREE

from the guided imagery exercises more so than from the mindfulness meditation.

Shannon: "The ones I did on my own were a bit superficial compared with the weekly sessions," she says. She was quite surprised to observe her ability to visualize "so clearly and vividly."

Bonnie: "The sessions were really good because she [the facilitator] talks you through and focuses you. I was surprised I found it far easier to visualize objects or words, so I would visualize anger or sadness rather than a sad scene."

Joel: "The guided sessions were quite profound. I could easily visualize and imagine the scenes in my mind. I was surprised at how vivid and detailed they were."

Mindfulness Meditation Practice

Daily mindfulness meditation practice was chosen to enhance an individual's ability to gain insight into the nature of the mind and, in doing so, help him or her observe and shift limiting beliefs and patterns of behavior, with the ultimate aim of eliciting a spiritual experience.

The participants' instructions for practicing mindfulness meditation involved holding one's attention on the inflow and outflow of the breath, with eyes closed. The participants were instructed to acknowledge any thought, sensation, or outer disturbance and return awareness to the breath.

CHAPTER THREE

All of the 11 participants experienced personal growth benefit from engaging in this practice, to varying degrees. To reiterate, 5 out of 11 participants did have spiritual experiences, which were all reported in their mindfulness meditation journals.

All participants noted that their ability to calm their minds improved over time, though in varying degrees. They also noted that, on specific days throughout the entire 8-week period, when there were immediate concerns or worries that calming the mind was more challenging.

Some of the most significant comments from the participants regarding personal growth they experienced pertaining to the mindfulness meditation practice include:

Amy: "I was thinking today of being more accepting of who I am and not play somebody else. I am not that bad after all, no matter what my hairstyle is and how much I earn. I want to love myself" and "In the meditations I could recognize it seems like logically everything seems fine but it doesn't work and it will come back to you if you don't do something about it. I see details that I didn't spot before. It increased my awareness."

Allen: "I feel more in control now as a result of the meditation. I am more in control of being myself—more contained. I would like to be with someone, but I don't feel desperate" and "before starting the meditation I found it difficult to wake up. I have a lot more energy to start my meditation in the morning. Now I don't even feel like staying in bed."

CHAPTER THREE

Kent: "Through the meditation I am learning to step back. I don't have to react or do anything at all" and "I'm thinking more about my spirituality and what that means to me."

Jenny: "I realized how full of details my head is. There were a few times that I got so inundated with thoughts of things I had to do or had forgotten that I had to jot them down on a piece of paper so that I could sit still. I noticed fewer distractions of this kind as the weeks went by. I cleaned up a lot of things really" and "I think that meditation is a fantastic practice for anyone that wants to learn to center themselves and to look at what they are doing."

Eva: "Since meditating, my outlook is more positive. I would have been a blithering mess, and the meditation has kept me going. I am able to slow down my thoughts down and express myself" and "I find that the meditation is helping me to deal with her [a person she has a relationship with] because I have to take several deep breaths before talking with her. Ordinarily something like that could really upset me, and although it's upsetting I'm dealing with it."

Jim: "There were a few times in the middle of the meditation where I was really struggling to get into a meditative place, and there were things constantly coming out so I actually went and did them to get them out of the way. Through that process I realized I should be doing that all the time" [not procrastinate] and "I want to invest more effort in the rest of my life. It gave me ideas to do that."

CHAPTER THREE

Joel: "I have developed a habit of breathing deeply whenever I think of it. I think that is a powerful tool for calming down" and "I enjoyed sitting quietly after the meditation with Stacey [his friend] sharing our experiences and the silence. Turning on the television didn't feel right" and "I can feel the difference between chaos and the joy of a still moment."

Shannon: "It helped me to take action. I was always taking the back seat. I wanted to get those things done. I became focused on things" and "I think it is his attention problem that has become sharper since the meditation [her awareness of someone else's behaviour]. It has also made me think about the repercussions" and "The meditation has given me time to clear out things that were going on and that are of no relevance and aren't going to get me anywhere."

Bonnie: "It makes you think about the most not-upfront-relevant stuff. I cried a few times and that worried me quite a bit really. I thought, 'I'm crying and I don't know what I'm crying about.' Other times I felt brilliant and I thought, oh this is really nice and I feel refreshed and I need to take this time more often. It fluctuated in the way it affected me" and "I have more of an attitude that things will be sorted but before I thought it was the end of the world."

David: "My focus has improved a lot not only in the meditation but in other areas as well. I have been experiencing general every day improvements such as reading more, and doing more for myself and not procrastinating. I am also more organized"

CHAPTER THREE

and "that there was a period where I missed a few days of meditation when I was travelling. It took me a couple of days to get back into it and when I did I immediately felt more calm and relaxed."

Frances: "I think it [her religious faith] is going along with the meditation which is helping me to let things be, and not get too concerned about them. Nothing I can do can change that so I just let it be and focus on myself" and "Since I have been doing the meditation I started to focus on my body more, and I am trying to think of things that are good for my health rather than bad for my health."

In addition to experiencing tangible personal growth benefits from the daily meditation practice, 3 of the 11 participants also became aware of the nature of their mind in a more expansive way. These 3 participants were all from the group who reported having spiritual experiences.

Amy: "I could see the difference when I noticed I was not thinking or I was thinking" and "One wonderful evening [in week 2] I saw clouds and that they didn't influence the sky as they were passing by" and "I think my mind is in a state of total mess but I think that this practice teaches me discipline" and "I sat and then thoughts came and I realized I actually stopped thinking."

Jim: "It's like having a closet in your mind that's full of disparate junk. It's all annoying if you let it build up" and "It's like the untidy closet. It's all the garbage floating around. It's not necessarily the good stuff or the important stuff. It's the nonsense stuff. If that's sorted out you can get to another place where your mind can be clearer" and "It's like my brain is a muscle and breathes itself" and "My mind kept filling with things I need to do. I must try and do a majority of them today so I can get them out of my mind."

Kent: "The daily meditation is an interesting practice. I seemed to go through different layers at different times. I found it interesting to notice the thoughts over time and the patterns of thoughts. It was also quite fascinating to be in the silence and darkness" and "Into week 5 or 6 it occurred to me that there is only stillness except for the thoughts I am thinking. When I don't think, nothing else exists" and "I found it easy to let thoughts go today as they came up. It reminded me of the sushi restaurants where the food dishes go by on a conveyor belt and you take the ones you want and let the others go by."

These same 3 participants who experienced the nature of the mind in a more expansive way were the same 3 participants who also experienced in excess of four spiritual experiences throughout the study.

Spiritual Experiences

The kinds of spiritual transformations that occurred for 5 of the 11 participants included the following experiences: altered states of consciousness beyond ordinary time/space awareness; the feeling of present-moment awareness; feelings of deep inner peace; feelings of blissfulness; and a sense of oneness or interconnectedness with objects of experience.

CHAPTER THREE

These experiences began to occur for the participants at different times throughout the study. Three out of 5 participants had four or more spiritual experiences, while 2 participants had fewer than four transpersonal experiences. Typically, the spiritual experiences were reported between the 5th and 8th week of the study.

Amy: "Then there was another time when I felt my heart beat and nothing else. Then I felt some heat in the energy going into my head and on my forehead. " In week 6 she wrote in her daily journal, "I had a moment when I felt blessed by the Holy Spirit. I saw myself in a golden triangle of light pouring from the top. I felt today my body as whole, as united." Also in her week 6 guided imagery journal she wrote, "I felt like I am separate from my body, kind of carrying it with me." Similarly in week 7, she wrote, "I had a vision of rays coming out of my head and connecting with God." Finally, in week 8, she wrote, "When breathing I realized how much we are a part of everything, and the air contains us and we contain the air. I had this great sensation on the crown of my head. I felt the blood pulsating on the top of my head and something pulling my head up."

Allen: "I got goose bumps a few times in my legs and head. It was instant. It was like a wave of energy going through my body that felt light and beautiful. It was amazing. I got it several times. Not goose bumps like being cold, but I could feel the energy move. It starts from the spine then head and legs and arms. [He started crying in the post-study interview when describing the experience again.] It took me to a new place. It helped me get closer to channeling, if you can call it that, or to

CHAPTER THREE

focus on it more. I just realized that by meditating I could connect more with the energy more than on a day-to-day basis. I could activate it through meditation and feel completely connected throughout the day. I have greater observation and calm." Week 4: "Today's meditation was peaceful too. I was in the present moment. Not too many thoughts came into my mind. I am feeling full of energy." Week 7: "Today I felt goose bumps moving through my spine, neck and head. It was a magical experience." Week 7: "Today was good. I meditated 10 minutes longer than I was supposed to. I had goose bumps this time. I suppose this means that I had a very strong connection with my energy source."

Kent: "Everything is space and we are part of the space too. Meditation makes me think of this. It's an illusion that most people relate to the world of objects. I want to know why it is this way, but I can't know because no one knows for sure," and "As the process continued by the week, maybe into week 5 or 6 it occurred to me that there is only stillness except for the thoughts I am thinking. When I don't think, nothing else exists. It is something I kind of thought but I never experienced directly. It's like being in deep space." Week 5: "I went into a deep space today. I felt a rush of energy in my neck and head. I felt weightless." Week 7: "I had an amazing session today. I felt out of body again. I lost track of the time completely."

Jenny: "Today was very peaceful. When a thought came in I could release it at will and return to my breathing. I felt in the moment with myself and my body. It was a very enjoyable experience." In one of her week 6 journal entries she wrote, "I feel grateful today that I am alive. I feel a sense of peace even though I have so many things to sort out. I know everything will work out and that there is a bigger plan for everything."

Eva: "I feel like singing its [meditation's] virtues to people. It's a wonderful thing. It's like a white light that fills you up inside" and "I experimented with myself towards the end [of the sessions] with being in the moment. I took 2 days to paint the flat and I thought of that as a meditation. I put myself there while I was covering these yellowing walls with white paint. I felt spiritual… it's probably not an exaggeration" and "It [the daily meditation] took a while to get into it—3 or 4 weeks. Sometimes I couldn't believe it's only been 2 minutes. When I am running around time goes quickly. When I was slowing down, time was going really slowly. But then after a while I thought that this is what I want. This is wonderful. This is happening right now" and "I am experiencing the silence. It really is beautiful."

Three of the 5 participants who reported having spiritual experiences, as stated above, also reported having intense sensations of energy moving through their bodies and heads. One of the participants who did not report any spiritual experiences also reported having these sensations of energy that he experienced as highly pleasurable, during some of his daily meditation sessions towards the end of the research period. I concluded from this that such experiences of energy sensation may also be a precursor to spiritual experiences. One participant who did not report having any spiritual experiences reported

CHAPTER THREE

the following:

Jim: "I swear to God I thought I could feel a hot breath on my face. It was like there was heat, like when the clouds go past and the sun bursts on to your face. It's almost like as a kid when you play with a puppy and his breath comes onto your face. It was lovely. I was very aware that it was happening. Almost to the point I wanted to open my eyes. I was trying to think 'what could this possibly be?' Things like that were really nice – tangible, calm and warmth."

Two of the participants from the group who did have spiritual experiences also reported a shift in self-identity that was spiritual in nature, from the pre-study interview to the post-study interview. In that sense, the practices had a cumulative effect that expanded their sense of self at the spiritual level, as opposed to remaining as isolated spiritual experiences in the mindfulness meditation practice. These post-study interview responses were:

Amy: "I know that I've got this divine part of me and I want to discover more of this and be connected all the time. I know it's there but I sometimes lose it. The meditation definitely helped me see new parts of myself. I am more kind of, in place. I am amazed."

Kent: "Everything is space and we are part of the space too. Meditation makes me think of this. It's an illusion that most people relate to the world of objects. I want to know why it is this way, but I can't know because no one knows for sure."

Only one participant who did report having spiritual experiences had the particular the type of spiritual experience known as nondual awareness. It is described as the experience of wholeness or the perceived unity of subject and object, such that there is no experiential differentiation of separate parts.

Amy: "When breathing I realized how much we are a part of everything, and the air contains us and we contain the air."

Conclusion

It was not necessarily the actual personal growth changes and spiritual experiences that the participants reported that surprised me. It was the speed with which they became more self-aware that surprised me. Through consistency and commitment these positive changes became possible. As well, it is amazing to me how conscious work on one's self in any area immediately enhances overall development.

It is also interesting that those who were able to quiet the activity of their minds through mindfulness meditation to experience sustained present-moment awareness were able to differentiate their Ego Self from their higher or Authentic Self.

CHAPTER FOUR

GUIDED IMAGERY VISUALIZATIONS

Here are eight guided imagery visualization exercises that you can use in conjunction with your meditation practice to enhance healing, self-observation, and self-awareness. It is best that you find a quiet place to sit down, close your eyes, and ask a friend or family member to very softly and slowly read through whichever exercise you feel drawn to. This is a silent inner process that you engage in with your mind's eye. It is highly recommended that you journal your experiences about the process afterwards as this helps you to remember and integrate any insights that may have come up for you during the session.

Some individuals are able to visualize more easily than others. This ability can be improved with practice and by specifically sensing into the detail of a particular mental image. For example, even if your visualization skills are not well developed, you can still call to mind an inner sense or picture of someone you know. Relaxing into the process with mindful breathing enhances receptivity.

The pacing of how the exercise is read aloud is an important aspect for fully engaging your inner process to give you enough time to properly visualize and mentally connect with your inner journey. Have a practice run with your reader to help him or her understand the correct pacing.

CHAPTER FOUR

1. Loss (letting go/rebirth)
2. Observer (accessing inner wisdom)
3. Tree Meditation (working through a challenging situation)
4. Talents (acknowledging talent/life purpose)
5. Inner Child (healing childhood memory)
6. Rhythm (flexibility/balance in life)
7. Ocean Wave (releasing/inviting new quality)
8. Future Vision (desired experiences)

Guided Imagery Visualization 1
Loss (letting go/rebirth)

(Read VERY slowly, with a soft voice, pausing in between each sentence, and longer where indicated.)

Sit comfortably with your feet flat on the ground, your hands resting gently in your lap, and close your eyes. Take several deep breaths of air: inhale relaxation and exhale tension, inhale relaxation and exhale tension, inhale relaxation and exhale tension. Relax the tiny muscles in your face, in your neck and shoulders, in your arms and legs, relaxing with each and every breath as you surrender into a state of acceptance and peacefulness.

You are walking in a beautiful and serene forest full of trees. Notice the many different sizes and types of trees, and the

CHAPTER FOUR

variety of plants and wild flowers. Ahead of you there is a ray of intense golden sunlight beaming through an opening in the trees. Walk towards this light and experience its warmth and brightness on your face. You are safe and protected in this natural environment. There is a deep sense of stillness and silence all around you.

Take a moment to connect with an aspect of your experience where an unexpected or difficult change brought with it the experience of loss, either around a person, or an object or something you had planned for the future. Take a few moments to identify this feeling of loss. (pause for 10 seconds) Allow yourself to connect with this sense of loss and the hurt associated with it. (pause for 10 seconds) Feel into self-compassion for the challenges of your journey.

Now sense into the newness of life around you—notice the new signs of life around you in the insect world, in the plants, and with the animals. Things are decaying to make space for the new. Connect with the new aspects of your life that are being birthed and the feeling they create within you. (pause for 7 seconds) How do you experience this newness in your body? (pause for 7 seconds) What opportunities does it represent for you? (pause for 7 seconds) What aspects of yourself are you letting go of in order to facilitate this positive change and growth? (pause for 10 seconds)

Breathe into this feeling and allow its truth to permeate every cell of your being. Take a few moments to acknowledge yourself and your feelings around your circumstances. (pause for 10 seconds)

Now imagine you are the tallest and widest tree in the forest. Connect with your roots and how deeply they weave into the ground. Feel your connectedness with the earth and the quality of solidness you possess. Feel the ever-present awareness and clarity you possess through all of life's changes. Breathe into this truth.

As I count from 10 to 1, slowly return your awareness to the room and open your eyes. 10, 9, 8, 7, 6, 5, 4, 3, 2, 1.

Take 20 minutes to write about your experience.

Guided Meditation 2

Observer (Accessing Inner wisdom)

(Read VERY slowly, with a soft voice, pausing in between each sentence and longer where indicated.)

Sit comfortably with your feet flat on the ground, your hands resting gently in your lap, and close your eyes. Take several deep breaths of air: inhale relaxation and exhale tension, inhale relaxation and exhale tension, inhale relaxation and exhale tension. Relax the tiny muscles in your face and around your eyes, relax the muscles in your neck and shoulders, in your arms and legs. Relax with each and every breath as you surrender into a state of acceptance and peacefulness.

Connect with the rhythm of your breath. Notice the inflow and

CHAPTER FOUR

outflow of each breath as you breathe deeply into your stomach and into your entire being. Feel your breath expand to awaken every cell in your body and feel your connection with the earth and everything around you.

Call to your awareness the part of you that observes life experiences both in your outer and inner world, the part of you that observes thoughts, feelings and perceptions as well as objects, people and situations. Allow the observer in you to take the form of a man or woman, a cartoon character, an animal or an object or symbol… let its form naturally arise in your mind without effort. (pause for 10 seconds) Feel into this image of yourself, your observer. Allow it to give you information or show you something that may be helpful to you in your life today. You may want to dialog with it. Take the next half minute to have this dialog (pause for 30 seconds)

Allow yourself to digest this information. What is it telling you to do or not to do? (pause for 15 seconds) How are you observing yourself in this moment as you receive this information? (pause for 10 seconds) Visualize yourself implementing this information in your life. How does it feel? (pause for 5 seconds) What do you see and hear? (pause for 5 seconds) Enter into the silence with this image and notice what it is saying to you about yourself.

Now allow your inner observer to change or morph into something different; allow this to happen naturally. Breathe into the visualization and feeling of this new form. (pause for 10 seconds) What is it trying to communicate to you about another

CHAPTER FOUR

aspect of your life? Allow yourself to receive the wisdom that is emerging as you dialog with this image inside yourself. (pause for 20 seconds)

Thank yourself for the wisdom that you have brought forth from inside of you. As I count from 10 to 1, slowly return your awareness to the room. 10, 9, 8, 7, 6, 5, 4, 3, 2, 1.

Take 20 minutes to write about what you experienced.

Guided Meditation 3
Tree (challenging situation)

(Read VERY slowly, with a soft voice, pausing in between each sentence and longer where indicated).

Sit comfortably with your feet flat on the ground, your hands resting gently in your lap, and close your eyes. Take several deep breaths of air. Inhale relaxation and exhale tension, inhale relaxation and exhale tension, inhale relaxation and exhale tension. Relax the tiny muscles in your face and around your eyes, relax the muscles in your neck and shoulders, in your arms and legs. Relax with each and every breath as you surrender into a state of acceptance and peacefulness.

Connect with the rhythm of your breath. Notice the inflow and outflow of each breath as you breathe deeply into your stomach and into your entire being. Feel your breath expand to awaken every cell in your body; feel your connection with the earth and everything around you.

CHAPTER FOUR

Now…call to your awareness a tree. Visualize this tree standing in a forest. How does it look? What are its characteristics? (pause for 7 seconds)

Now see yourself stepping into this tree to become a part of it. Feel your roots deeply intertwined into the earth as you connect with your groundedness. Sense into the solidness of your trunk and branches as you connect with your ability to move and bend. Feel the wind blowing around you. (pause for 5 seconds) You have lived for many years and endured many challenges that have made you stronger and more resilient.

Bring to mind a current life challenge you are facing. (pause for 7 seconds) Where do you feel this challenge in your tree body? How does this challenge make you feel? (pause for 5 seconds) You are now aware that a bird has come to land on one of your branches. What kind of bird is it? (pause for 5 seconds) What are its qualities? (pause for 5 seconds) This bird represents the wisest part of you…the part that knows how to be and what to do when needed. What is the bird communicating with you about your situation? (pause for 15 seconds) How are you receiving this information? (pause for 5 seconds) As you sit in silence feel into the wisdom of your own being as you hold your ground in the presence of this challenge. You know exactly what you need to do or not do in this situation in order to bring it closer to a resolution. Visualize your challenge changing its form. How it is playing out in your life? Create this scenario with as much detail as possible. (pause for 15 seconds)

CHAPTER FOUR

The wise part of you, the bird, is always there for you to call upon at any time you want. Breathe in a sense of gratitude for this part of yourself. Now visualize yourself stepping out of the tree. While you have mobility, you remain connected with your groundedness. Feel into your connection with the earth with your feet on the ground, and tune in to your ability to ground in knowing what is right for you. Breathe deeply into this knowing...

As I count from 10 to 1, slowly return your awareness to the room. 10, 9, 8, 7, 6, 5, 4, 3, 2, 1.

Take 20 minutes to write about what you experienced.

Guided Meditation 4
Talents (acknowledging talent/life purpose)

(Read VERY slowly, with a soft voice, pausing in between each sentence and longer where indicated.)

Sit comfortably with your feet flat on the ground, your hands resting gently in your lap, and close your eyes. Take several deep breaths of air: inhale relaxation and exhale tension, inhale relaxation and exhale tension, inhale relaxation and exhale tension. Relax the tiny muscles in your face and around your eyes, relax the muscles in your neck and shoulders, in your arms and legs. Relax with each and every breath as you surrender into a state of acceptance and peacefulness.

Connect with the rhythm of your breath. Notice the inflow and outflow of each breath as you breathe deeply into your stomach,

CHAPTER FOUR

into your entire being. Feel your breath expand to awaken every cell in your body; feel your connection with the earth and everything around you.

Now...call to your awareness a particular talent or gift that you possess that you feel may be under-utilized. (pause for 10 seconds) As you connect with this talent, allow it to take a visual form like a symbol or object or living form. (pause for 10 seconds) Connect with this form and the feeling it awakens inside of you. (pause for 5 seconds) What is the quality of this feeling? (pause for 5 seconds) What does it feel like to acknowledge this gift you possess? (pause for 10 seconds)

Now visualize yourself expressing this talent in your life. Allow the details of this vision to take form with great detail, particular people and places and situations where you are expressing this particular talent. Take some time to create this vision. (pause for 15 seconds) How are others responding to you? What are they saying? (pause for 10 seconds) How are you responding? (pause for 10 seconds)

Take another few moments to be with this vision and breathe into the feelings of acceptance and gratitude.

As I count from 10 to 1, slowly return your awareness to the room. 10, 9, 8, 7, 6, 5, 4, 3, 2, 1.

Take 20 minutes to write about what you experienced.

CHAPTER FOUR

Guided Meditation 5
Inner Child (healing childhood memory, strengthening self)

(Read VERY slowly, with a soft voice, pausing in between each sentence and longer where indicated.)

Sit comfortably with your feet flat on the ground, your hands resting gently in your lap, and close your eyes. Take several deep breaths of air: inhale relaxation and exhale tension, inhale relaxation and exhale tension, inhale relaxation and exhale tension. Relax the tiny muscles in your face and around your eyes, relax the muscles in your neck and shoulders, in your arms and legs. Relax with each and every breath as you surrender into a state of acceptance and peacefulness.

Connect with the rhythm of your breath. Notice the inflow and outflow of each breath as you breathe deeply into your stomach, into your entire being. Feel your breath expand to awaken every cell in your body; feel your connection with the earth and everything around you.

Now picture yourself as a child. How old are you? What does your face look like? What does your hair look like? (pause for 5 seconds) Now I'd like you to allow yourself to recall one of the challenges you faced as a child. Allow a specific memory to come to mind. (pause for 15 seconds) Connect with how this challenge made you feel as you visualize yourself as a child. (pause for 7 seconds) Allow your heart to open with compassion for the hurt that you experienced. (pause for 10 seconds)

Now allow yourself to connect with the wisest part of you.

CHAPTER FOUR

What can this wise adult say to your inner child in this moment? (pause for 15 seconds) How is your inner child receiving this information? (pause for 10 seconds) Take a few moments to love and accept this vulnerable part of yourself. (pause for 10 seconds)

Now re-direct your awareness with your connection to the earth and the feeling of groundedness. Feel both of your feet and the weight of your body on the ground. Breathe into this feeling several times and as I count from 10 to 1, slowly return your awareness to the room. 10, 9, 8, 7, 6, 5, 4, 3, 2, 1.

Take 20 minutes to write about what you experienced.

Guided Meditation 6

Rhythm (maintaining inner balance)

(Read VERY slowly, with a soft voice, pausing in between each sentence and for longer where indicated.)

Sit comfortably with your feet flat on the ground, your hands resting gently in your lap, and close your eyes. Take several deep breaths of air: inhale relaxation and exhale tension, inhale relaxation and exhale tension, inhale relaxation and exhale tension. Relax the tiny muscles in your face, in your neck and shoulders, in your arms and legs. Relax with each and every breath as you surrender into a state of acceptance and peacefulness.

Connect with the rhythm of your breath. Notice the inflow and

CHAPTER FOUR

outflow of each breath as you breathe deeply into your stomach. Feel your breath expand to awaken every cell in your body and feel your connection with the earth and everything around you.

Now bring your attention to your mind and the rhythm of your thoughts as they flow in and out of your awareness. (pause for 7 seconds) As each thought arises allow it to pass gently from your mind. (pause for 5 seconds) Now allow an image or picture of this movement to form in your awareness. What do you see? (pause for 10 seconds)

Sense into the push and pull of experience that is always present in your life, the people you meet that come and go. Who are the faces that come to mind? (pause for 10 seconds) Now sense into the feelings that come and go from moment to moment in your experience. How do you feel this rhythm in your body? (pause for 5 seconds) Notice the rise and fall of your body as you breathe (pause for 5 seconds)

Now connect with the part of you that maintains balance through the changes of life experience. Allow this wise part of you to take the form of a wise person. What does that part of you look like? What are you wearing? (pause for 10 seconds) Let this wise part of you share its wisdom around maintaining your rhythm and balance through life's highs and lows.

Call to mind any area of your life that requires balancing. (pause for 5 seconds) Breathe into it and allow yourself to adjust perfectly. Feel into your energy as it moves inside your body; sense into where you feel this change the most. (pause for 5

CHAPTER FOUR

seconds) Allow these shifts to speak to you about any necessary outer adjustment you need to make in your experience to facilitate this balancing. (pause for 15 seconds)

Take a moment to feel gratitude for this wise and intuitive part of yourself (pause for 10 seconds). Now feel into the ground under your feet and the weight of your body on the earth. You are grounded in yourself.

As I count from 10 to 1, slowly return your awareness to the room. 10, 9, 8, 7, 6, 5, 4, 3, 2, 1.

Take 20 minutes to write about what you experienced.

Guided Meditation 7
Ocean Waves (releasing/inviting new quality)

(Read VERY slowly, with a soft voice, pausing in between each sentence and longer where indicated.)

Sit comfortably with your feet flat on the ground, your hands resting gently in your lap, and close your eyes. Take several deep breaths of air: inhale relaxation and exhale tension, inhale relaxation and exhale tension, inhale relaxation and exhale tension. Relax the tiny muscles in your face, in your neck and shoulders, in your arms and legs. Relax with each and every breath as you surrender into a state of acceptance and peacefulness.

Connect with the rhythm of your breath. Notice the inflow and

CHAPTER FOUR

outflow of each breath as you breathe deeply into your stomach. Feel your breath expand to awaken every cell in your body and feel your connection with the earth and everything around you.

Now imagine yourself walking alone along an expansive beach that stretches for miles in each direction. Feel into the wind, and the sun, and the sand. What time of day is it? How do you feel in this moment? (pause for 5 seconds) Find a comfortable place to sit and face the ocean. Connect with the sound of the waves. Allow yourself to sense into the power of the ocean and its waves. Perhaps a particular feeling or physical sensation comes to mind...

Now think of a personal quality or habit that you feel may not be serving you. (pause for 5 seconds) Imagine this quality becoming a physical form or symbol. What do you see? (pause for 5 seconds) Allow the ocean waves to pull this symbol or form out to sea. Take a few moments to visualize and feel into this picture. (pause for 10 seconds) Now imagine how different your life is without this quality. Visualize yourself with as much detail as possible living life without this quality or habit. (pause for 15 seconds) Take a moment to breathe into the feeling of gratitude...

Now think of a personal quality or habit that you would like to cultivate or invite into your life experience. What comes to mind? (pause for 5 seconds) Imagine this quality becoming a physical form or symbol that has meaning for you...what do you see? (pause for 5 seconds) Now the ocean waves are washing this symbol or form onto the shore. Imagine it fusing fully into your being. How does this make you feel? (pause for 10 seconds) Imagine living your life with this quality. How are you expressing it? (pause for 10 seconds) How are people responding to you? (pause for 10 seconds) Take a moment to breathe into the feeling of gratitude as you acknowledge the beauty of this magical moment.

Take several more moments to feel and experience yourself in this new way. As I count from 10 to 1, slowly return your awareness to the room. 10, 9, 8, 7, 6, 5, 4, 3, 2, 1.

Take 20 minutes to write about what you experienced.

Guided Meditation 8

Future Vision (Desired Experiences)

(Read VERY slowly, with a soft voice, pausing in between each sentence and longer where indicated.)

Sit comfortably with your feet flat on the ground, your hands resting gently in your lap, and close your eyes. Take several deep breaths of air. Inhale relaxation and exhale tension, inhale relaxation and exhale tension, inhale relaxation and exhale tension. Relax the tiny muscles in your face and around your eyes; relax the muscles in your neck and shoulders, in your arms and legs. Relax with each and every breath as you surrender into a state of acceptance and peacefulness.

Connect with the rhythm of your breath. Notice the inflow and outflow of each breath as you breathe deeply into your stomach

CHAPTER FOUR

and into your entire being. Feel your breath expand to awaken every cell in your body and feel your connection with the earth and everything around you.

Now visualize yourself emerging from the edge of a forest. Connect with the expansiveness of the sky. How does it look? (pause for 5 seconds) What is the mood it evokes in you? (pause for 5 seconds) Feel the wind as it blows against your face and body. Tune into any sounds that surround you. What do you hear? (pause for 5 seconds)

In the distance you see a mountain. Visualize how this mountain looks and the qualities it has. (pause for 7 seconds) Now you notice a path that leads to the mountain. This path represents your future—it is open and receptive to whatever you would like it to be. You are free to pursue the things in life that hold meaning for you. You feel the spaciousness and opportunity of this moment.

You are walking along the path towards the foot of the mountain. Allow yourself to connect with the unlimited potential of the future and how it makes you feel. It is now a short time into the future. You are experiencing something significant that you set out to do. Visualize this experience with as much detail that you can imagine. (pause for 15 seconds) Connect with the joy and sense of satisfaction that this experience is creating for you. (pause for 10 seconds)

You continue walking and arrive at the base of the mountain. You stop and take a moment to enjoy the scenery and the

CHAPTER FOUR

anticipation of what lies ahead on your journey. (pause for 5 seconds) You stretch out your arms and take a deep breath of air as you begin your ascent up the mountain. You notice different terrain in different areas and rely on the strongest part of you to make it past the difficult parts of the climb. Eventually you reach a clearing on the mountain side with a view point. You see that you have climbed a good distance up the mountain. It is now further into the future. You are experiencing something significant that you set out to do. Visualize this experience with as much detail that you can imagine. (pause for 15 seconds) Connect with the joy and sense of satisfaction that this experience is creating for you. (pause for 10 seconds)

You feel a deep sense of gratitude and personal accomplishment. You take one last look out into the horizon, acknowledging the beauty of life and your commitment to yourself.

Now you begin the final climb up the mountain side to the top. As you continue to put one foot in front of the other you make steady progress. You feel strong and alive. As you glance over your shoulder and look down the mountainside you see how far you have come. Take a moment to acknowledge yourself.

As you continue to climb you feel that you have worked your body well. Take a moment to acknowledge your efforts and commitment to keep going. Honour the part of yourself that is strong and capable. (pause for 5 seconds) In a few more steps you reach the top of the mountain. At the peak you walk all around and see out into every direction. What do you see?

CHAPTER FOUR

(pause for 5 seconds) It is now even further into the future. You are enjoying amazing success in your life. You are experiencing something significant that you set out to do. Visualize this experience with as much detail that you can imagine. (pause for 15 seconds) Connect with the joy and sense of satisfaction that this experience is creating for you. (pause for 10 seconds)

Your friends, family and associates are congratulating you. (pause for 7 seconds) Allow yourself to fully receive the joy and abundance that has come into your life. (pause for 7 seconds) Feel the gratitude for everything you have attracted, acknowledging the people in your life who supported you.

As you look out over the mountain you see and experience the beauty of life. You are acknowledging your proactive spirit to consciously direct your experiences. Yes!! You did it!!

Take a few more moments to fully receive all that you have created for yourself. As I count from 10 to 1, slowly return your awareness to the room. 10, 9, 8, 7, 6, 5, 4, 3, 2, 1.

Take 20 minutes to write about what you experienced.

CHAPTER FIVE

SITTING PRACTICES: BASIC STEPS

Preparation

Apart from the times you may practice activity-based meditations, your core sitting meditation practice should be in a place that is free from distraction so that you can truly quiet your mind. It is recommended that you make a sacred space for yourself to help establish your practice as a valued routine in your life. You could light a candle or have flowers or an object that has meaning for you close by. It is also helpful to a set a specific time each day to meditate. A good time is in the morning when you are rested. You can also have a session in the evening to help you unwind and clear your mind at the end of your day. Twice a day is recommended, with at least one 30-minute session. You can begin with 5 or 10 minutes and gradually increase it.

You could sit on the floor or in a straight-backed chair, using the base of the backrest as a support to your lower back as you sit tall with your spine straight, yet relaxed. This aids in comfortably positioning your body for maximum energy flow. It is recommended that you close your eyes. If you feel more comfortable leaving them open it is helpful to face a wall to limit outer visual distractions. It is also possible to meditate lying down, though initially this may hinder your understanding of the process as it becomes very easy to fall asleep.

CHAPTER FIVE

Working with Tension

When you feel tension arise in your body it can be challenging to quiet your mind. This is why many people do not stay with the practice… it can be uncomfortable both mentally and physically. However, it is this very tension that represents the creation of energy. This energy can be used to move you forward to allow you to rest naturally in a quiet and aware state. In other words, rather than perceive the tension you feel as a barrier to moving forward, it is energy that you are working with that can serve to accelerate your movement forward.

If you can remain steadfast in the face of any tension you might feel, and breathe through it for as long as possible, the tension may increase at first before you feel a release into a more relaxed state. The longer you can focus on remaining in the present moment, the sooner you will break through the tension and experience that same energy in a new way. It will be completely free of tension and can be highly energizing. Ideally, you could practice both mindfulness meditation and concentrative meditation – one in the morning and another later on in the day.

The concentrative practice of single-pointed focus using sound I recommend as the first practice that you learn, as this form of mental training, by virtue of its simplicity may be easier to learn and experience 'quiet mind'. Once you 'get it' it should be easier to flow into the mindfulness meditation practice.

CHAPTER FIVE

Learning Mindfulness Meditation

1. Find a comfortable place to sit down free from distraction.
2. Sit with your spine straight, yet relaxed, with your hands open and resting in your lap or by your side.
3. Close your eyes and place your attention on the inflow and outflow of your breath.
4. When a thought comes into your awareness, acknowledge it without following it or reacting to it and let it go, returning your awareness to your breath. Same with sensations or feelings.
5. Practice non-judgement around any thought that comes up.
6. Hold your awareness in the present moment using your breath.

CHAPTER FIVE

Concentrative Practice

Concentrative meditation is about cultivating single-pointed focus on a specific object of meditation such as sound, physical object, mental image or your breath. While mindfulness practice allows all objects of experience to be sensed in the moment, the concentrative approach is about holding unwavering attention. Focus is the point of the exercise as it gives the mind a simple task to do, and as it becomes automatic and fixed it creates a space for present-moment awareness to be experienced. To reiterate, it is easier for many to learn concentrative practice first, and integrate mindfulness meditation practice afterwards. Start with a few minutes a day and build on your practice, ideally working up to one 30-minute session a day.

Choosing Your Focal Point

Mental image – choose any mental image to focus on, perhaps something that has particular interest to you or meaning for you. It is much easier to practice this with your eyes closed as you have fewer distractions. Similar to mindfulness meditation, when a thought comes into your awareness, simply acknowledge it and let it go without judgement, returning your focus to your mental image. One mental image might be of a tree, a flower, or the image of a person you love or admire.

Physical object – choose a physical object that has some significance for you, if possible, and position it in a space that allows you to focus on it without the distraction of other objects.

CHAPTER FIVE

You could place the object on a small table against the wall, for example, and sit close enough to it for you to easily focus on it. If other thoughts come to mind as you are beginning the process, simply acknowledge them and return to your point of focus.

Breath – I personally prefer to use the breath as my focal point. You may have your eyes open or closed, though there are fewer distractions when they are closed. Place your focus on the movement of each breath, following it along the inflow as it increases to its natural resting point, and maintain your awareness on it all the way through the outflow, and back again. I typically elongate my breathing at first as I am settling in the practice and then let it find its own natural rhythm, which is usually quite a bit slower. Try to keep your inhale and exhale of the same duration, closing the back of your throat slightly to release the breath at a slower, steady pace.

Sound or mantra – You can choose any type of sound, word or phrase in this practice. If you want to keep it simple, choose any vowel sound – A, E, I, O, or U and sound it out loud, taking in an adequate breath (into your lower abdominal area) and exhale while making the sound you have chosen. Obviously if you are repeating your sound, word or phrase (mantra) out loud you are also following the path of the breath in and out. You can also hear the sound internally without actually making a sound. Once the word or phrase is repeated a few times it becomes automatic and effortless. I tend to use a mantra or particular phrase that has meaning for me when I am intending to create or attract something specific into my experience.

CHAPTER FIVE

Learning Concentrative Meditation

1. Find a comfortable place to sit down free from distraction.
2. Sit with your spine straight, yet relaxed, with your hands open and resting in your lap or by your side.
3. Close your eyes and place your focused attention either on your breath, the sound, image or object you have chosen to work with.
4. If you are using a mantra, repeat the sound or phrase, aloud or silently, in continual succession.
5. Practice non-judgement around your experience.
6. Hold your awareness in the present moment by focusing your attention on your sound repetition (or object).
7. Let your breath find its own natural rhythm.

CHAPTER FIVE

Manifesting Your Desires

It is believed that through the repetition of a particular word or phrase that the intention or quality behind the mantra is infused into the life of the individual practicing it. For example, there are mantras for attracting wealth, friendship, creativity, peace, removing obstacles etc. "The primary mechanism of creation is sound," says Thomas Ashley-Ferrand, author of *Healing Mantras*: using sound affirmations for personal power, creativity and healing. The mantras in the book are written in Sanskrit language as this is the language that the Eastern ancient practices used in India. The book also teaches you how to pronounce the words properly. Once you repeat them a certain number of times, it gets easier.

The book states that you can practice these mantras during any type of activity – while you are walking, doing daily chores etc. For the purpose of learning sitting meditation however, it is critical to sit down and repeat the mantra in your daily practice to quiet your mind. If your intention is also to create or attract something specific into your life using sound and intention, you can take extra time outside of your sitting practice to repeat your mantra. Here are a few examples from the book:

CHAPTER FIVE

To Remove Obstacles
Om Gum Ganapatayei Namaha.
(om gum –guh-nuh-puh-tuh-yei nahm-ah-ha).

To Remove Fear of Loneliness and Attract Companionship
Om Hraum Mitraya Namaha.
(om hrouwm mee-trah-yah nahm-ah-ha.

To Attract Abundance
Om Sri Maha Lakshmiyei Swaha.
(om shree mah-ha laksh-mee-yei swah-ha).

For Creating Peace
Om Shanti Om.
(om shahn-tee om).

For Spiritual Growth
Om Nama Shivaya.
(om nah-mah shee-vah-yah)

I AM Affirmations

The words 'I Am' have a particularly powerful affirming quality, which is why it is important to attach positive intentions to them. You can also create your own mantras in whatever language you desire. You can tailor them to your specific desires.

CHAPTER FIVE

Here are some examples:

I am.

I am love.

I am courage.

I am confidence.

I am aware.

I am joy.

I am peaceful.

I am healing or I am healthy.

I am mindful.

I am focused.

I am living abundantly.

I am strong and flexible.

I am receptive to life.

I am secure in myself.

I am free.

I am alive.

They can also be longer and more detailed:

I am gratefully accepting and appreciating my life.

I am effortlessly experiencing health and healing.

I am effortlessly making conscious choices.

I am effortlessly enjoying abundance in every area of my life.

I am one with myself, others and nature.

I am at peace with everything regardless of its outer form.

I am easily and effortlessly completing the tasks I have set for myself.

I am easily and effortlessly expressing my creativity.

I am gratefully appreciating my vitality and aliveness.

I am easily and joyfully enjoying my interaction with others.

I am acknowledging ever-present stillness amid the experience of disturbance.

I am effortlessly maintaining present-moment awareness.

I am resting in the beauty and perfection of eternal quiet mind.

I am that I am, an open, receptive and loving human being.

The ultimate value of life depends upon
awareness and the power of contemplation
rather than upon mere survival

ARISTOTLE

If reading this book has changed your life or perspective, please email your experiences to:

WhatHappened@jainwells.com

NOTES

NOTES

NOTES

NOTES